Marie Hedderwick Browne

A Spray of Lilac

And Other Poems And Songs

Marie Hedderwick Browne

A Spray of Lilac
And Other Poems And Songs

ISBN/EAN: 9783744713375

Printed in Europe, USA, Canada, Australia, Japan

Cover: Foto ©Thomas Meinert / pixelio.de

More available books at **www.hansebooks.com**

A Spray of Lilac

And Other Poems and Songs

BY

MARIE HEDDERWICK BROWNE

LONDON
ISBISTER AND COMPANY Limited
15 & 16 TAVISTOCK STREET COVENT GARDEN
1892

*Oh, lilac bloom! strange that so slight a thing
As thou is strong to roll away the stone
From memory's grave, and set the dead past free
To claim again brief kinship with its own.*

PREFATORY NOTE

Most of the Poems contained in this volume have appeared during the past ten years, in "Atalanta," "Chambers's Journal," "London Society," "Little Folks," "The Girl's Own Paper," and other serials.

If an apology for venturing to offer them to the public in collected form be deemed necessary, I can only urge the plea of the poor but hospitable Dervish, "He is a generous host who freely giveth his best, be his best but clear water and a crust."

M. H. B.

London, December 1892

CONTENTS

	PAGE
A SPRAY OF LILAC	1
IN AN OLD GARDEN	3
A MOTHER'S GRIEF	5
A SUMMER MEMORY	8
UNSATISFIED	11
MY SONG	12
IN AN OLD CHURCHYARD	13
SECRETS	15
REVEALED—NOT SPOKEN	16
BURIED TREASURES	19
AFFINITY	20
"MY HOUSE IS LEFT UNTO ME DESOLATE"	21
AN OLD MAN'S DREAM	22
A SUMMER WOOING	24
WEE ELSIE	26
BIDE WI' MITHER	28
CHILD ANGELS	30
MY LOVE OF LONG AGO	32
IN SUMMER TIME	34
TWIN-SISTERS	36
AT LAST	38
TRYSTING-TIME	40
BESIDE THE DEAD	41
HER FIRST SEASON	43
ANTICIPATED	46
WHEN THOU ART NEAR	47
A PORTRAIT	48
DOROTHY	49
DAFFODILS	51
THE BLACKBIRD	52
"WHOM THE GODS LOVE DIE YOUNG"	53
GRANNIE'S BAIRN	54
LOVE'S POWER	56

Contents

	PAGE
A JUNE MEMORY	57
A MESSAGE	59
HER WINDOW	61
SHATTERED HOPES	62
HAND IN HAND	64
"AND FOR THE WEARY, REST"	65
IN AN OLD ORCHARD	67
BY THE SEA	68
REGRET	69
WAE'S ME	70
THE REASON WHY	71
DOWN BY THE SEA	73
A VENTURE	74
WATER LILIES	75
THE SENTINEL	76
A LOVE SONG	77
AUTUMN	78
A QUAKER MAID	79
THE TIME, THE PLACE, THE BELOVED	81
DAY DREAMS	82
SONG OF THE SEASONS	83
ONE SUMMER DAY	84
THE INSCRUTABLE	85
DELILAH	86
A BABY'S GRAVE	87
A CHILD'S FAVOURITE	88
RICH OR POOR?	89
DOLLY'S GARDEN	90
IN A DREAM-SHIP	91
THE FLOWER-QUEEN'S FALL	93
A VETERAN	95
TO A BUTTERFLY	96
WHEN AND WHERE	96
WHEN LOVE IS YOUNG	100
A CHARACTER SKETCH	101
FRIENDS	102
BED-TIME	104

A SPRAY OF LILAC

PALE cluster, thy faint perfume comes to me
   Laden with memories of long ago,
And all the present dims as o'er my soul
   The waves of tender recollection flow.

With Spring's young blood again my veins are thrilled,
   My hands are stretched to meet the coming years,
The world holds all the glory that it held
   Ere yet mine eyes had looked on it thro' tears.

With deftest fingers fancy weaves once more
   Her fairy fabrics; vast horizons glow
With fires of promise, for behind their veils
   They hid rich treasures in that long-ago.

A

The subtle sweetness of the vanished days,
   The rapture of the old ecstatic bliss,
All, all are mine, as once again I cling
   To ripe warm lips in love's first passion-kiss.

The long delicious Summer slowly weaves
   For Autumn's brows a crown of living gold;
Sad Winter follows with his winding-sheet,
   For all the glory has grown grey and old.

Oh, lilac bloom, strange that so slight a thing
   As thou, is strong to roll away the stone
From memory's grave, and set the dead past free
   To claim yet once brief kinship with its own.

IN AN OLD GARDEN

Yellow roses, purple pansies,
  Tufts of heavy-headed stocks;
Either side the quaint old gateway
  Blazing, torch-like hollyhocks.

Sweet peas tossing airy banners,
  Saintly lilies bending low,
Daisies, powdering all the green sward
  With a shower of summer snow.

Boxwood borders—yews fantastic—
  Wallflowers that with every sigh
Spill such scent that e'en the brown bees,
  Reel with rapture wandering by.

And the pear trees, long arms stretching
   O'er the sunny gable wall,
Scarce can hold their ruddy nurslings
   Ripening where the warm beams fall.

Oh, the ecstasy of living!
   How it thrills my life to-day!
I can almost hear the flower-bells
   Tinkle where my footsteps stray!

In a garden God first placed man,
   There first woke Love's magic thrill;
And methinks a breath of Eden
   Clings to earth's old gardens still.

A MOTHER'S GRIEF

To a great wide city all alone,
    Long, long ago went our baby queen—
No name but hers on the white headstone,
    That gleams to the moon from its mound of green!
None of her own did welcome her there—
    Not a grain of kindred dust doth wave
In the flowers that out of the tears of despair
    Have arched a rainbow over her grave.

Out from the shelter of loving arms,
    Out from the warmth of a mother's breast,
Heedless of darkness and night's alarms,
    On to the silent city she pressed
To take her place 'mong the mighty throng
    That people its myriad streets. Ah, me!
I felt my God had done me a wrong,
    When He loosened love's cords and set her free!

And my passionate moan that broke in tears,
   Like a burdened wave on a desert shore,
Seemed all too feeble to reach His ears
   And the pain grew old that my bosom bore;
But the faith that I once had thought mine own
   Rose up to mock where it could not save,
And my heart grew hard as the carven stone
   That was crushing my darling in her grave.

Whenever a child's sweet flower-like face
   Met mine, a sickness would o'er me creep,
And I'd turn wild eyes to the lonely place
   Where she was lying alone—asleep.
At strife was I with the world, and God
   Had drawn around Him an angry cloud;
Earth held no green but the churchyard sod,
   And the daisies wore the gleam of a shroud.

But a time there came when about my breast
   With a wand'ring touch small fingers stole,
And feeble lips to its fountains pressed,
   And stirred with a vague sweet joy my soul;

A Mother's Grief

And the floodgates opened, and blessèd tears
  Of repentance fell from my eyes like rain,
And after the barren and prayerless years
  I knelt to the Giver of All again!

A SUMMER MEMORY

I REMEMBER an evening,
   An evening in one far June,
The sun seemed loth to leave the sky
   To a young impatient moon.

The yellow sands lay waiting
   For the sea's long cool embrace;
We watched the ripples breaking,
   Like smiles upon its face.

The green trees nestled closer
   To the broad breast of the hill;
The twilight's glamour gathered,
   And the day was with us still.

And a sadness born of beauty,
    And a joy to pain akin,
Touched all that lay without us,
    And hushed my soul within.

A silence stepped between us,
    We seemed to stand apart;
Yet I thought your eyes grew tender,
    And I know what filled my heart.

But the words were never spoken;
    And the distance wider grew,
Till the world of waves was lying
    Between me, love, and you,

No bridge might ever cross it.
    I watched you turn away,
And I went back to duty—
    'Tis all a woman may.

But I never shall be nearer
    The thrilling heights of bliss—
Unless the next world gives us
    The love we lose in this—

Than when in that far June-time,
  We seemed to stand apart,
And I thought your eyes grew tender,
  And I knew what filled my heart.

UNSATISFIED

Oh, "dear dead days" that dearer grow,
   I look behind, and thro' my tears,
   Across a wide, wide gulf of years,
I see you now and now I *know*.

When I was yours, you mine, alas!
   I did not know your real worth,
   And, longing for the future's birth,
Found time so slow, so slow to pass.

The joys I hoped for never came,
   While those I held slipped from my clasp,
   As I stretched yearning hands to grasp
Shadows—'tis evermore the same!

We strain dim eyes up to the stars,
   Nor heed the blossoms at our feet;
   Like puny birds we beat and beat
Our lives out 'gainst Fate's prison bars.

MY SONG

"When love is mine," said I, "I'll make a song
   In praise of love that maketh life so sweet;
One worthy such a grand and noble theme—
   Worthy to lay at my belovèd's feet.

"Pure, perfect pearls of poesy I'll string
   On Music's silken thread, so rhythmic-sweet
That those who hear shall feel as though each word
   Were but an echo of my heart's warm beat."

Now love *is* mine; but where my boasted song?
   My heart is full—too full, ah me! for words;
And yet methinks my new-found joy has lent
   Fresh rapture to the voices of the birds.

And I am dumb; the world will never hear
   The music filling all this life of mine.
Oh! love is too sublime a theme for me;
   I can but kneel in silence at love's shrine.

IN AN OLD CHURCHYARD

In one of England's sweetest spots,
    A little old grey church I found;
    Around it lies—dear restful ground!
God's garden with its sacred plots.

With myriad arms the ivy holds
    Its time-worn walls in close embrace:
    So Memory sometimes keeps a face
Half-veiled in tender misty folds.

With sleepy twitter and with song
    The tower, bird-haunted, is alive;
    In leafy seas they dip and dive,
Those tiny warblers all day long.

Like sentinels grown hoar with age,
    The crumbling headstones guard the graves
    Which softly swell—green voiceless waves
That will not break though tempests rage.

"Concerning them that are asleep"
   In this sweet hamlet of the dead,
   In broken sentences I read
The record those old tablets keep;

Each told its tale, for hath not Grief
   A voice whose echoes never die?
   Adown the ages, Rachel's cry
Still rings o'er some God-garnered sheaf.

Mine eyes, ne'er prodigal of tears,
   Did fill with such as seemed to rise
   And drown the glory of the skies,
O'er those who'd slept the sleep of years.

SECRETS

July roses wet with rain
Tap against the window-pane;
There is something they would seek,
Had they voices and could speak.
Silence seals their crimson lips,
And the dull rain drops and drips.

Th' other side the streaming glass
Stands a little sad-eyed lass;
There is something she would seek,
But a maiden may not speak—
Silence seals her longing lips,
And the dull rain drops and drips.

And salt tears in showers stain
Her side of the window-pane;
And the crimson roses grow
Pale as dreams dreamt long ago;
(Hearts may break behind sealed lips),
And the dull rain drops and drips.

REVEALED—NOT SPOKEN

THE little maiden that I love,
  I met in yonder lane;
A flood of sunshine seemed to fall
  Around her as she came.

Methought the very hedgerows took
  A tenderer, livelier green,
And blossoms burst from every bud
  As she passed on between!

And gladder, madder, merrier notes
  A skylark round him threw,
As high above her golden head,
  He poised amid the blue.

Revealed—Not Spoken

I meant to tell her all my heart,
    And yet—I know not why,
Upon the threshold of my lips
    The story seemed to die.

It might have been the witchery,
    The magic of her smile,
That in a spell held all my soul,
    And kept me dumb the while!

It might have been that all too pure
    For earth-born love seemed she;
From her white height of maidenhood
    How could she stoop to me?

But eyes can prove more eloquent,
    And though the tongue may fail,
In potent language they reveal
    The old, old tender tale.

For, placing her slim hand in mine,
    Methought I heard my name
So softly, murmurously breathed,
    I scarce knew whence it came!

No need for words between us now;
   A subtle sweetness stole
Through all our being, and we felt
   That soul had answered soul.

And with the sunshine in our hearts,
   The bird's song in our ears,
We left the lane, my love and I,
   To meet the coming years.

BURIED TREASURES

'Tis true my later years are blest
    With all that riches can bestow,
But there is wealth, wealth cannot buy,
    Hid in the mines of "Long Ago."

There jealous guard does Memory keep;
    Yet sometimes, when I dream alone,
She comes and takes my hand in hers,
    And shows me what was once my own.

I revel 'mong such precious things;
    I count my treasures o'er and o'er;
I learn the worth of some, whose worth,
    Ah me! I never knew before.

And then all slowly fades away,
    And I return to things *you* know,
With empty hands and tear-filled eyes,
    Back from the mines of "Long Ago."

AFFINITY

But little converse have we held,
   Our hands have scarcely ever met,
With just a formal word or two
   You come and go; and yet—and yet—
I have a dream we two were one
   Ere garb of flesh these spirits wore;
The soul that speaks within your eyes
   Tells mine they've met and loved before.

And so I am content to wait,
   Knowing the day will surely dawn
When, as the first man woke, you'll wake
   From your soul-sleep, and looking on
My face will know that I am she,
   Your Eve, your other self, your fate.
Till then, till then, come weal or woe,
   I am content, content to *wait*.

"MY HOUSE IS LEFT UNTO ME DESOLATE"

A LITTLE while, you say, a little while,
  And I shall be where my belovèd are;
And with your eyes aglow with faith, you say,
  "Thy dear ones have not journeyed very far."

"Not very far." I say it o'er and o'er,
  Till on mine ear mine own voice strangely falls,
Like some mechanic utterance that repeats
  A meaningless refrain to empty walls.

"Not very far;" but measured by my grief,
  A distance measureless as my despair.
When from the dreams that give them back to me,
  I wake to find that they have journeyed there!

"Not very far." The soul surmises, hopes,
  Has hoped, surmising, since the first man slept;
But, oh, the heart, it knoweth its own loss,
  And death is death, as 'twas when Rachel wept.

AN OLD MAN'S DREAM

With idle hands and misty eyes,
   I sit alone to-night and dream ;
Upon the hearth, like elfin sprites,
   The red flames dance, and twist, and gleam.

A dimness gathers in my room,
   The pictured faces on the wall
Pale, and o'er each familiar thing
   A strangeness slowly seems to fall.

With noiseless step there comes to me,
   One whom I loved in days gone by.
The same is she, unchanged by time—
   Unchanged—but oh, how changed am I !

An Old Man's Dream

Her hair, which long, long years ago
   Was like spun threads of living gold,
Still clusters round a brow that wears
   Immortal youth—and I am old.

No look of recognition lights
   Her eyes, that meet mine o'er and o'er;
And yet she loved me once—and love,
   I know, is love for evermore.

She looks around in anxious quest;
   I think I know for whom she seeks.
She only sees a strange old man,
   With snow-white hair and wrinkled cheeks.

And then like wings of birds that preen
   For flight, a soft stir moves the air,
It is the whisper of her gown—
   She goes to look for me elsewhere.

A sudden glory fills my eyes,
   It is the firelight's ruddy gleam;
Thank God she did not pass me by
   I only saw her in a dream!

A SUMMER WOOING

A SONG

Up and away!—up, up, and away!
The hedgerows are foaming with blossom to-day;
Its bonfires the golden gorse lights on the hill,
And the wanton wind's wooing wherever it will.

Up and away!—up, up, and away!
The cuckoo's name rings through the woodlands to-day;
The warm blood of Summer runs rioting through
The veins of each leaflet—then why not of you?

Up and away!—up, up, and away!
There's Passion and Poetry stirring to-day.
Half blinded with rapture, the heavy bees dart
From the lily's white breast to the rose's red heart.

Up and away!—up, up, and away!
The old world's begun a fresh courting to-day.
I wooed you all winter, but found you as cold
As the snowdrift that gleamed on the ridge of the wold.

Up and away!—up, up, and away!
Your eyes tell me "Yes," though your lips say me "Nay."
The tears, so long frost-bound, are ready to flow,
And she melts in my arms, my proud maiden of snow!

WEE ELSIE

O' a' the bonny wee bit lasses
That e'er I've kent, not ane surpasses
    My Elsie.

An' oh, she has sic denty ways,
Auld farrant a' she does and says ;
Just watch the bairnie as she plays
" At mither," dressed in mither's claes !

Like twa sweet rosebuds on ae stalk,
Her lips part in her guileless talk ;
She hauds a key that wad unlock
Yer heart were't hard as granite rock.

Sae fearless are her een o' blue,
They seem tae look ye through an' through ;
But though sae brave, an' frank, an' true,
Wi' happy fun they're brimmin' fu'.

Adoun her shoulders floats her hair,
Sae long, sae silken, an' sae fair,—
In truth it seems a verra snare
That's caught an' kept a sunbeam there.

But better faur, those graces meet
Aroun' a nature just as sweet˙;
Methinks the bairnie is complete
Frae wise wee heed tae willin' feet.

BIDE WI' MITHER

Oh bide a wee, my bonny lass,
Nor seek to lea' the auld hame-nest;
O' a' earth's luvs ye yet will fin'
A mither's highest is, an' best.

She watched you like a rose unfauld,
She reads you like an open buik;
You scarce need speak, she is sae quick
Tae understan' yer ev'ry luik.

The han' that aye fan' time tae pat
The wee bit face sae aft turned up
For "mither's kiss," has workit late
An' early for your bite an' sup.

An' oh! it was a struggle sair
Tae mak' twa unco scrimp en's meet;
In her first days o' weedowhood
She scarce could spare the time tae greet.

Oh dinna lea' her yet awhile;
The laddie's young, an' he can wait;
There was a time, when you were wee,
She micht hae had anither mate.

But she was feert he micht na be
As guid's the fayther you had lost;
An' though she could hae boucht her ease,
She wad na' dae it at the cost.

An' noo she's auld an' growing frail,
Your strong young arm should be her stay;
Life's dounward slope is hard eneuch,
Be yours the han' tae smooth the way.

Oh, bide wi' her, an' you will fin'
That duty done brings sweet reward;
The Maister, Christ, pleased na' Himsel',
Although He was creation's Lord!

CHILD ANGELS

Oh, there are happy angels
   That go on missions sweet;
They have no wings to bear them,
   Just little human feet.

When I had grown aweary,
   And all my faith was dim,
'Twas one of them that led me,
   And brought me back to Him.

When 'tween you and a loved one
   There lay a widening breach,
And you were coldly drifting
   Beyond each other's reach,

Child Angels

A child's hand 'twas that bridged it—
 A child's soft, rosy palm
Held both your souls united,
 And life grew sweet and calm.

When sorrows closely gathered,
 And heart and head were bowed,
The blue eyes of a baby
 Made rifts in pain's dark cloud.

Oh, happy, earth-born angels,
 Who go on missions sweet,
If ye had wings to bear you,
 Instead of little feet,

I fear me ye would use them,
 Altho' ye love us much,
To soar to Him who tells us
 His "Kingdom is of such."

MY LOVE OF LONG AGO

There are faces just as perfect;
  There are eyes as true and sweet;
There are hearts as strong and tender
  As the heart that's ceased to beat;
There are voices just as thrilling;
  There are souls as white, I know,
As hers was when she went from me—
  My love of long ago.

New lips are ever telling
  The tale that ne'er grows old;
Life's greys are always changing
  For some one into gold;
But amid the shine and shadow,
  Amid the gloom and glow,
She walks with me, she talks with me—
  My love of long ago.

My Love of Long Ago

When I think of all the changes
    That the years to me have brought,
I am glad the world that holds her
    Is the world that changes not.
And the same as when she left me,
    She waits for me, I know—
My love on earth, my love in heaven,
    My love of long ago.

IN SUMMER TIME

DAISIES nod and blue-bells ring,
Streamlets laugh and song birds sing,
To the clover bees close cling.

Cornfields wave their locks of gold,
Poppies burn and wings unfold,
Earth-stars twinkle on the mould.

Butterflies—live blossoms, blown
From that Eden once our own—
Make of every flower a throne.

And a royal purple dyes
Yonder heather-hill, that lies
Fitting footstool for the skies.

In Summer Time

And the gorse is all ablaze,
Lighting up the moorland ways,
And the days are golden days.

E'en the myriad-mooded sea
(Earth-bound, yet than earth more free)
Wears a look of *constancy*.

And your love, that in the spring
Was a shy, uncertain thing,
Like a bud just blossoming,

With the summer's growth has grown,
Till our two lives, lived as one,
Make a summer of their own.

TWIN-SISTERS

Two girls—before me now they stand,
Twin tender rosebuds, hand in hand,
Fashioned as one—scarce known apart;
I see each face, God sees each heart.

I look on ripe red lips, and eyes
That hold the blue of summer skies,
And hair like finest gold refined;
I see the beauty, God the mind.

In womanhood's first faint sweet dawn
Oh! they are fair to look upon;
Perfect from crown to dainty foot;
I see the bloom, God sees the fruit.

Twin-Sisters

What though a rose is each soft cheek,
If theirs be not that spirit meek?
What though their eyes are heaven's own hue,
If never wet with pity's dew?

The plainest casket may enshrine
A gem that will for ever shine.
Oh, may this outward beauty be
But type of inward purity!

God grant when Time its tale hath told,
And backward swing the gates of gold,
Before the Master they may stand,
Twin tender rosebuds hand in hand!

AT LAST

She is waiting for his coming,
   As she waited long ago,
Ere her sweet eyes were pain-haunted
   Or her hair was touched with snow;
Ere that look of patient pathos
   Downward curved her tender lips,
Or across her life's young morning
   Fell a shadow of eclipse.

He is coming—but his footsteps
   Know not now youth's bounding grace,
And a world of sin and suffering
   Is recorded in his face;
Airy dreams of high ambition
   That he cherished in the past—
All have vanished—and aweary
   He returns to her at last.

At Last

In the old familiar garden
   Where he first breathed love's fond vow,
With new hopes, like the new roses
   Sprung from old roots, they stand now;
And the past is past for ever,
   She forgives, and he forgets,
For the present peace has buried
   Years of sorrows and regrets.

TRYSTING-TIME

'Tis only when the wooing west
Has drawn the tired sun to her breast,
I seek my darling's place of rest.

In twilight-time we used to meet—
Ah me, how lag our listless feet
When we have but a grave to greet!

And yet, this daisy-dappled grave
So like a soft white-crested wave
Is all beneath the skies I have.

On broken wings the years have flown,
Oh love, since in the long agone
I left you sleeping here alone!

BESIDE THE DEAD

Touch not her hand, let not your tear-drops stain
   The show-white purity of her dead brow;
Withhold your lips, their passion or their pain
   Can thrill her nor with love nor pity now.

The empty years that followed your farewell—
   The joyless dawns, the nights that brought no rest
Are ended,—and those weary eyelids fell
   O'er eyes that had grown dim in one vain quest.

Thank God for this; her woman's faith remained
   Steadfast, unshaken to the very last,
And with her idol undefaced, unstained,
   To place it in a "niche in Heaven" she passed.

But yesterday, your lightest whispered word
   Had thrilled her heart, as spring's first breath awakes
The rapture in the bosom of a bird
   Till winter's silence with a song he breaks.

And I,—whose love for her was purified
   In the fierce crucible of human pain,
Had felt that I was more than satisfied
   If loss of mine had ended in her gain.

For her soul's sustenance you only left
   The memory of a lightly plighted vow,
To take one kiss from those dead lips were theft,
   The jewel was yours,—I claim the casket now.

HER FIRST SEASON

CLOUD-LIKE laces softly float
Round a dainty snow-white throat—
Fastened here and flutt'ring there
With a careless cunning care;
Blue-bells, blue as summer skies are.
Or her own sweet sunny eyes are,
Cluster close beneath her chin,
As if love—and not a pin—
Kept them fondly nestling in!

Gown of some transparent thing,
Like a dragonfly's clear wing
Full of whispers vague and sweet,
Falls in white folds to her feet.

Light as moss veils drape their roses,
Round her flower-like form it closes—
Every graceful curve it shows us.

Silken mittens soft and quaint,
Of a shade æsthetic, faint,
Weave a jealous network o'er
Two pink palms that I adore;
And a musical mixed jangle
Comes from bracelet and from bangle
As it fetters each slim wrist
(Made but to be clasped and kissed),
With fantastic coil and twist.

Hair a-ripple like ripe corn
Wind-kissed on a summer morn.
What, you say you see the glint
Of a reaper's blue scythe in't?
Nay, 'tis but a silver arrow
Wand'ring through a golden furrow,
Where the sun-shafts bore and burrow.

Her First Season

Like a bright plumed bird is she,
From the home-nest just set free;
Knowing neither grief nor wrong,
In her heart and lips a song.
"Tis not I would wish to make her
Prim and drab-gown'd like a Quaker!
All fair things are beauty's dower—
Doth not God's hand paint the flower?
(Youth is but a fleeting hour!)

ANTICIPATED

Oh I have wealth, and could have placed
   Upon your head a golden crown,
But Nature, having had my taste,
   And being first, has set one down.

I could have given you rubies rare,
   And sapphires of a heavenly hue,
And pearls all shimmering soft and fair;
   But here she's been before me too.

For ruby lips to you she's given,
   And strung two pearly rows between,
And sapphire eyes more blue than heaven
   She's dowered you with, my queen, my queen!

I needs must be content to lay
   My heart's best treasures at your feet:
Without love's gem, which shines for aye,
   The fairest crown were incomplete.

WHEN THOU ART NEAR

A SONG

When thou art near no other face I see,
   Thy voice is all the music I can hear;
My heart's desire is granted unto me
   When thou art near.

When thou art near I am content, nay more,
   I'm blest in breathing the same atmosphere.
To higher heights my aspirations soar
   When thou art near.

When thou art near, though yet I dare not lay
   My lips on those I hold so very dear,
I know that heaven is not so far away
   When thou art near.

A PORTRAIT

A SADNESS lingers round her lips,
   A shadow ever haunts her eyes;
Like dusky pools are they on which
   The mystery of the moonlight lies.

Her voice is sweet, but grave in tone,
   No ring hath it of joyous mirth;
Yet somehow when she speaks, methinks
   A benediction falls on earth.

A sense of rest her presence brings,
   She moves with such a quiet grace;
And 'tis the pitying soul within
   Makes tender twilight of her face.

Methinks the Virgin-mother must
   Have looked like this when to her breast
The Babe, who was to save a world,
   With mingled joy and pain she pressed.

DOROTHY

Dorothy is debonair;
Little count hath she or care;
All her gold is in her hair.

And the freshness of the Spring
Round this old world seems to cling
When you hear her laugh or sing.

On her sunny way she goes;
Much she wonders—little knows,
Love's as yet a folded rose.

All her smiles in dimples die;
Glad is she, nor knows she why:
Just to live is ecstasy!

Lightly lie the chains, methinks,
That have daisies for their links;
Youth's the fount where Pleasure drinks.

Dorothy is debonair;
Little count hath she or care,
Sunshine in her heart and hair.

DAFFODILS

Oh, wild is the daffodils' dance
   To the tune that the March pipes blow,
Heads a-tossing—lances crossing,
   Curtsies sweeping and low.

Like waves in a flaming sunset
   They tumble, and twist, and turn,
What tho' from its slender pillar
   Droppeth one golden urn?

Short-lived is their joy and reckless,
   Never a pause for breath.
Ah, well!—are *we* too not whirling
   As blind, in our "dance of death"?

THE BLACKBIRD

When baby buds begin to shoot
Then hey! the blackbird's golden flute;
All steeped in love seems every note
Let loose from his mellifluous throat.

No wild rhapsodic bursts proclaim
What rapture thrills his tiny frame,
His heart is like a brimming cup,
Where pearls of joy keep bubbling up.

The lark like some delirious thing
At heaven's far gate may soar and sing,
But oh, methinks the blackbird brings
Heaven down to earth what time he sings!

"WHOM THE GODS LOVE DIE YOUNG"

HER voice is hushed, her hands are still,
I, from the summit of the hill,
Look down, and marvel at God's will.

Her foot was planted at the base
All eager for the upward race,
Her genius shining in her face.

She felt the soul within her leap,
She yearned to scale the steepest steep,
And now—she's fallen upon sleep!

God knoweth best!—I must descend
The downward slope. Good-bye, sweet friend,
Life's myriad ways meet in the end.

GRANNIE'S BAIRN

When oor wee Elspeth's in the hoose
    I scarce hae use for hauns or feet—
An' after a', why *should* I fash
    When she's sae nimble an' sae fleet?

"I wonner whaur I laid my specs!"
    The words hae haurdly left ma mooth
Afore I fin', across my nose,
    She has them set astride forsooth.

She threeds ma needle, winds ma woo',
    Picks up the steeks that whiles *will* drap—
She slips aboot like some wee moose
    For fear she'll wauke me frae ma nap.

Grannie's Bairn

Her wee three-leggit stool ye'll aye
   Fin' drawn up close tae granny's chair;
She learns her task an' sews her seam,
   An' sups her cog o' parritch there.

An' mony's the lang crack we twa hae;
   But whiles, sic puzzlin' things she'll spier,
The verra Meenister himsel'
   Waud be dumbfounded could he hear.

She *has* her bit camsterie turns,
   But just eneuch tae show that she
Is no a being that is made
   O' diff'rent clay tae you an' me.

But that she's no by-ord'nar wean
   The neebors roon aboot agree,
And sae ye ken it is na just
   Ma *ain* opeenion that I gie.

LOVE'S POWER

When you did leave me, love,
The whole world seem'd with you to ebb away,
And like a broken stranded wreck I lay.

But you returned; and lo!
A fresh tide thrill'd my life's deserted shore;
And Love was conqueror over Death once more.

A JUNE MEMORY

'Twas June, the roses were reigning
   In regalest splendour and pride.
Sweet peas, like butterflies tethered,
   Were flutt'ring on every side.

Like smouldering fires the wallflowers
   Burned dull in the sun's strong glow,
And the yellow bees, like meteors,
   Went flashing to and fro.

No lordly pleasaunce was it,
   But an old-world garden wild,
Where purple-hooded pansies
   And long-lashed daisies smiled.

And there in June we parted;
   And the sad years hurtle by
Like birds whose wings are broken
   When they just have learned to fly.

And I think,—Do you remember
   In the life that's yours to-day,
That garden and its glamour,
   And the time that *would not* stay!

Oh, amid the faces around you,
   Does one face never arise
And for a moment hold you
   With the old spell of its eyes?

Ah no! You men forget us,
   And we!—we must be dumb.
And life's June goes for ever
   And the snows of winter come.

A MESSAGE

In a little broken flower-pot
  High up on a window-sill,
'Mid grime and gloom and squalor,
  Grew a golden daffodil.

It seem'd in the gloom of the alley
  Like a sunbeam that had strayed
Out from the light of heaven
  Into a land of shade.

And close in a cage beside it
  A skylark sweetly sang
Till all the narrow alley
  With its wild rapture rang.

And one poor weary sinner
    Paused, as her wild eyes turned
To where, on its humble altar,
    The flower-flame upward burned.

And something stirred in her bosom;
    'Twas the heart that had long lain dead,
As the bird's song rose from its prison
    In the shadow overhead.

God's angels are birds and flowers,
    And oh! methinks they preach
At times with a power and pathos
    We men can never reach.

HER WINDOW

Up the gable the roses creep,
Eager to get a little peep
Behind the curtain of snowy lace
That hangs, like a bridal veil, over the face
Of a shy wee window, whose panes glint through
A network of creepers, like eyes of blue.

I needs must stand below, below,
And see them high and higher go
Till their lips are kissing the lattice sill,
And their tendrils toy at their own sweet will
With the casement, so full of tender charms
Since *her* shadow has lain within its arms.

SHATTERED HOPES

This morn upon the birken tree
The mavis carolled blithe and free;
But—ah, his song was not for me!

Each wild note of his glad refrain
Pierced like an arrow thro' my brain;
I could have cursed him for his strain.

I saw the sunshine and the flowers,
Each proof of a Creator's powers;
Yet dull and hateful were the hours.

I cannot weep—the fever dries
The tears within my burning eyes—
The past before my vision flies.

Shattered Hopes

Once more I feel his deep-drawn kiss ;
Once more my being thrills with bliss ;
Once more I melt with tenderness.

I hear the trembling words that hung
Deep fraught with passion on his tongue,
Till heart and soul with pain are wrung.

All nature smiles—and yet to-day
In memory's grave I've laid away
My idol that has turned to clay.

HAND IN HAND

HAND in hand through the flow'ry ways
Went Dora and I in the bygone days;
A wee girl she, her boy lover I,
Ready to fight for her and die.

Hand in hand through this vale of tears
Went Dora and I in the after-years;
She was my wife and her husband I
Ready to fight for her and die.

Hand in hand to the very last
As her dear eyes dimmed, and her spirit passed;
An angel is she,—alone am I
Ready, O, God! and I *cannot* die.

"AND FOR THE WEARY, REST"

Of all God's precious promises
   The sweetest and the best
Is, that to weary laden ones
   Who come, He giveth *rest*.

'Tis not of glad Hosannas
   And streets of shining gold
We think so much when we are sick
   And sorrowful and old.

Ah! there are times we feel too sad
   To contemplate the joy,
The great and glorious themes of heaven
   That angel-minds employ.

And weak, and worn, and weary,
    We long to lay us down,
Feeling we scarce could bear the weight
    Of e'en a glory-crown.

That He is "very man," I need
    None other proof than this,—
That He has "rest" for those who feel
    Almost too tired for bliss.

IN AN OLD ORCHARD

Sweet avalanches of scented snow
Bury one deep, as I lie below
The laden white boughs abloom and ablow
In the dear old orchard, where long ago
My grand-dame dreamed, as I'm dreaming now,
With love in her heart and youth on her brow.

O, blossom-time passes too soon, too soon!
And grey night follows the golden noon,
And Autumn though ruddy brings ruin and rune,
And passion ne'er warms the cold heart of the moon.
So let me dream on, 'mid the apple-blooms sweet,
For noontide and bloomtide are fair as they're fleet.

And then when the blue of the sky is o'ercast,
And Summer is ended, and harvest is past,
And the loosened leaves earthward are fluttering fast,
And the sleep that is dreamless is mine at last,
O, make my grave here; and lay me to rest
Where the sweet-scented snow shall fall light on my breast.

BY THE SEA

I THINK, as the white sails come and go,
Of the welcomes loud, and the farewells low;
Of the meeting lips, and the parting tears,
Of the new-born hopes, and the growing fears,
Of the eyes that glow, and the cheeks that pale,
As the hazy horizon's mystic veil
Is silently parted, and to and fro
The white sails come and the white sails go.

And a grey mist gathers, and all grows dim
As I watch alone by the ocean's rim.
For a dream is mine—ah me! ah me!
That salt with *tears* is the salt salt sea.
O, yearning eyes and outstretched hands!
O, divided lives, and divided lands!
As long as the waters ebb and flow
Shall the white sails come and the white sails go.

REGRET

"It might have been," is the sad refrain
That forever haunts my weary brain,
Till heart and soul grow weak with pain.

"It might have been," are the words I hear
In the curlew's cry from the lonely mere;
In the whisper of leaves when woods are sere.

"It might have been," says the sea's long moan,
As if a breaking heart of its own
Wailed out in that strange low undertone.

"*It might have been.*"   Ah, the hungry cry
As the leaden years crawl slowly by!
It will ring through my life till I die, I die.

WAE'S ME

Aroun' my bit bieldie the cauld win' is soughing,
   The dull rain is patt'ring amang the deid leaves,
The mist-wreaths are swirling about the grey mountains,
   The wee drookit birds huddle close 'neath the eaves.

Alang the bleak shore the lane sea gangs a sobbin'
   Like some wander'd bairnie that fain wad win hame,
Aye seekin' an' seekin', an' never yet findin',—
   Sure man, in his pilgrimage here, is the same.

The sky has nae promise, the earth hauds nae pleesure.
   I look north an' south, an' I look east an' west,
An' I envy the folk i' the kirk-yaird out yonder,
   For there, 'mang the mools, there is rest—there is rest!

THE REASON WHY

I KEN the lassie's winsome,
    An' blithe as she is braw;
But 'tis not worth nor beauty aye
    That steal the heart awa'.

Her cheek is like the wild-rose,
    Her lips are like the haw;
But neither ane nor t'ither 'twas
    That stole my heart awa'.

Her locks are black as midnight,
    Her brow like driven snaw;
And yet it was na' these I vow
    That stole my heart awa'.

Her smile is like the sunshine,
    'Twad gar an iceberg thaw;
But 'twas na' this by my guid-faith
    That stole my heart awa'.

Ilk lad's lass the fairest is,
    For Beauty kens nae law;
(Though *some* folk maun be easy pleased
    Wha's hearts are stown awa'!)

Ah weel! maybe the pearl I've foun'
    Is no wi'out a flaw!
But just because she's her ain sel'
    She stole my heart awa'.

DOWN BY THE SEA

O, MIGHTY organ of a thousand keys,
   O'er which the Master's fingers ever stray!
I, listening, hear a myriad melodies
   Played in the space of one short summer day.

The long, low plash of little languid waves,
   The sweet, sad dirge of softly dying swell,
The deep, delicious gurglings in the caves,
   Hold music that this soul of mine loves well.

Full as the human heart of mysteries,
   Like it responsive to His touch alone,
For only He can wake the harmonies
   Which sleep within thy bosom and mine own.

A VENTURE

HER mouth looks like a scarlet flower
   And I feel like a hungry bee,
I long to dart straight to its heart,
   But—what would be the fate of me?

The bravest 'tis should win the prize,
   And yet I dare not risk her scorn,
And who but knows the reddest rose
   May hide the very sharpest thorn?

Yet who can tell but she might yield
   Its sweetness up in one long kiss?
So I, who dare not risk her scorn,
   Can risk still less to lose such bliss.

And when she feels my parchèd lips
   Athirst with long long years of drouth,
She will forgive me, that I sought
   That dewy chalice, her sweet mouth.

WATER LILIES

A FLEET of fairy vessels
　All freighted with pure gold,
The lilies lie at anchor
　On the lake's breast, calm and cold.

Their soft, white sails, seem waiting
　The zephyr's first faint kiss
To waft them to another world,
　More bright and fair than this.

Methinks, it were no marvel,
　If I should find, one day,
They'd drifted from their moorings,
　And in silence sailed away.

THE SENTINEL

"Tick! tick! tick!" goes the old clock in the hall;
　The merry hours, the mournful hours
Alike he counts them all
　　As he stands erect at his post,
　　Time's solemn Sentinel.

All that he hath to say he saith,
　And on, with never a pause for breath,
He hurries us nearer the day of death.
Though his warning voice is ofttimes drowned
　In the whirr, as the wheels of life run round,
Yet, whether or no we *hear* the sound,—

"Tick! tick! tick!" goes the old clock in the hall;
　The merry hours, the mournful hours
Alike he counts them all,
　　As he stands erect at his post,
　　Time's solemn Sentinel.

A LOVE SONG

Upon a bosom snowy white
   A little dimpled chin drops down,
While trembling shy lids hide the light
   Of love, new born in eyes dark brown.

A tiny timorous hand seeks mine
   For shelter, fluttering like a dove;
And with a rapture half divine
   I burn my kisses through its glove.

June's rosy treasures sweetly blend
   Upon her cheek and modest brow,
But only Cupid's self could lend
   The crimson stealing o'er them now.

Her voice makes music of my name,
   A heaven of love is in her smile,
Her pure mind, like an altar-flame,
   Burns clear and steady all the while.

AUTUMN

Red as blood is Autumn's gown,
And a flaming fire her crown.

And her fingers sere and scorch,
Each one a destroying torch.

Fever follows in her wake,
Nor the dews her thirst can slake.

In her kisses there is death,
And decay in every breath.

She makes tombs of what were bowers,
Strewn with corses of dead flowers.

To the loftiest leaves that wave
She but whispers of a grave.

A QUAKER MAID

Just a pair of green-grey eyes,
   With a knack of changing
Like the sea, when shine and shower
   O'er its breast are ranging.

Just a pair of green-grey eyes
   Each one a heart-breaker,
Who would think that they belonged
   To a little Quaker?

Prim her bonnet, drab her gown,
   And she walks sedately,
With a sort of lily-mien—
   Drooping, and yet stately.

And her voice sounds, oh, so meek!
 "Thou" and "thee" and "thying,"
Yet the while those grey-green eyes
 Seem to be belying.

All these airs of calm repose,—
 This sad suit and sober,
Why *should* Spring's young sapling be
 Brown-leaved like October?

Gown her in the lilies' white!
 Crown her curls with roses!
Wreath her neck with daisy-chains!
 Fill her hands with posies!

Laughter-loving green-grey eyes,
 Young limbs girt with gladness,
How they mock this dismal drab
 Livery of sadness!

"THE TIME, THE PLACE, THE BELOVED."

You and I among the roses—
    You and I and love and June—
All without and all within us
    Set to one sweet happy tune!

You and I among the roses!
    Drowsy bees go blundering by;
'Mid the tresses on your temples
    Little breezes swoon and die.

You and I among the roses!
    Overhead a sapphire dome;
'Neath our feet a sea of emerald,
    Flecked with daisies for its foam.

You and I among the roses—
    'Tis for love the time and place!
What a world of rapture can be
    Crowded into one small space.

DAY-DREAMS

I am dreaming of you, belovèd,
  In my home among the hills;
Your eyes meet mine in every flower;
Above the highest height you tower,
Yet the glamour of your presence
  The lowest valley fills.

I hear your voice in the river
  That sings on its way to the sea;
And when the wind sweeps over
The low beds of the clover,
'Tis the breath of my belovèd
  Its wide wings bear to me.

I am dreaming of you, belovèd,
  But though sweet these day-dreams be,
'Tis the deeper dreams of sleeping
That restore you to my keeping,
And so the world of shadows
  Is the dearest world to me.

SONG OF THE SEASONS

Sing, oh sing, 'tis summer time!
    Sing it 'mong the roses,—
Sing it till each sleeping bud,
    Dewy-eyed, uncloses.

Sing it through the woodlands, till
    All the song-birds hear it!
Sing,—till every blade of grass
    Finds a voice to cheer it.

   *   *   *   *   *

Sigh, oh sigh, 'tis winter drear!
    Sigh it through the flowing
Shroud that over earth's dead breast
    Falls in time of snowing.

Sigh it through the bare brown stems
    That once held the roses!
Sigh it round the grave, that o'er
    Summer's glory closes.

ONE SUMMER DAY

THE sky stretched blue above us,
   The sea slept at our feet,
As still, as if its mighty heart
   Had almost ceased to beat.

A trembling hush seemed slowly
   Across the earth to steal,
As when after benediction
   The priest and people kneel.

It was as though God's finger
   Lay on the pulse of life,
And stilled, for one brief moment,
   Its tumult and its strife.

THE INSCRUTABLE

A GLAD young girl amid the sunshine flitting,
   Like a bright bird let loose from Paradise—
A weary woman, in the shadow, sitting
   With haggard face and dry despairing eyes.

    *   *   *   *   *   *

The one in death's dark chamber now is lying,
   Stricken to marble her warm pulsing breast:
And God denies the luxury of dying
   To the sad soul whose one cry is for *rest,*

DELILAH

Why comest thou with those grand eyes of thine
   To lure me as the cruel light the moth,
   To my destruction.—Long ago my wrath
Cooled its white heat in pity's depths divine.

There was a time when full of bitter hate
   I could have crushed thee—but that time is past,
   And tho' I needs must love thee to the last,
Tempt me not now—it is too late, too late.

Apart for evermore our paths must lie,
   Such love as thine can only bring a curse.
   I would be better for my love, not worse,
So go while I have strength to say "Good-bye."

A BABY'S GRAVE

I could not lay her down to sleep
   In a death-crowded place,
With grim black yews to keep God's sun
   From shining on her face.

With softest greenest moss I lined
   For her a little nest;
No crushing marble slab I laid
   Upon her tender breast.

Nor iron rails like prison-bars
   Her sacred form enclose,
The sternest guardian of her grave
   Is just a fragile rose.

A CHILD'S FAVOURITE

ONLY an old wooden dolly,
   With an arm and a leg a-missing,
The point of her nose rubbed off, I suppose,
   Through too much washing or kissing.

In a frock of faded satin,
   With tinsel lace tarnished and tattered;
Her "coal-scuttle" bonnet holds, alas!
   A head that's a trifle battered.

Oh, no, she has not lost her locks,
   She *never* had curls black or golden;
A doll's wig was safely painted on
   In the days that *you* call "olden."

You laugh, and think her "too funny;"
   Yet *once* she was just as much cherished
As *your* dolly is—by a wee girl
   Whose dolly-days long ago perished.

RICH OR POOR?

Only a string of cold white pearls,
   Or diamond drops, like frozen tears,
Has clasped my lady's slender neck
   Through all the barren empty years.

Only wee warm white baby arms
   Have clasped *my* neck thro' the sweet years;
Yet she is rich and I am poor—
   Or so it to the world appears.

DOLLY'S GARDEN

This is Dolly's garden,
   All her "very own,"
Every flower that's in it
   By her hand was sown—
Never out of Eden
   Were such blossoms blown.

Like her eyes those pansies,
   Deep and dark and blue—
As her soul those lilies,
   Pure and white and true;
Frail earth-flowers and fading—
   Dolly's fading too.

This *was* Dolly's garden,
   Here I stand *alone*,
Dolly's tending blossoms
   Near the Great White Throne:
Dolly now has heaven
   For her "very own."

IN A DREAM-SHIP

SHE sailed away one summer day
   In a ship of shining shell:
Her cloak was a butterfly's gauzy wing,
   Her bonnet a big blue-bell,
Her bed was a lady's slipper,
   Her blankets the leaves of a rose,
And a cushion of thistledown had she,
   Just to rest her tiny toes.

With golden oars from the earth's dark shores
   She was borne o'er a silver sea;
And she never feared as the captain steered
   For the land where she wished to be.

   And this was the song,
   As they drifted along,
That she sang from the ship of shell—

"Oh, we are bound
For enchanted ground;
It's *there* that the fairies dwell."

But a storm swept over the silver sea,
   And the little maid awoke
As against the side of the fair frail barque
   A cruel billow broke;
And she rubbed her eyes, and she pinched her arm,
   And fearfully peeped around;
But instead of a ship "for fairyland"
   She had boarded a "homeward-bound."

THE FLOWER-QUEEN'S FALL

A REBEL rose climbed to the top of the hedge,
   And watched the people go up and down
The winding highway, dusty and grey,
   That stretched from the village away to the town.

And an anger surged in her passionate heart,
   'Gainst the humble garden where she was born,
And her red lips curled at the old flower world,
   And she cast around her such looks of scorn

That the lilies drooped 'neath her withering glance,
   And the pansies huddled together with fear,
And the poor pinks paled, and each daisy quailed,
   And dropped from her lashes a big round tear.

For of the flower-kingdom this rose was queen,
   And never were subjects more loyal than they—
And they fondly dreamed she was good as she seemed,
   And because they had loved they were proud to obey.

But lo! as she towered in haughty disdain
   High over their heads, with an angry gust
The wind swooped down and tore off her crown,
   And its jewels went whirling away with the dust.

A VETERAN

In his niche in the hall, the old clock stands,
But hushed is his voice, and still are his hands.
He ceased from his labours long years ago,
And he's only a "pensioner" now, you know.

He did his duty as long as he could,
For a brave heart beat in his breast of wood,
And you could depend on *all* he said
Till age, at last, turned him queer in the head.

With a visor of glass o'er his grim old face,
In his armour,—a straight, stiff, oaken case,
He "stands at ease" in his sentry box,
And leaves time-telling to younger clocks.

TO A BUTTERFLY

Butterfly, O butterfly,
  With gaily-jewelled wings,
You make me think of fairy folk
  And of enchanted things.

You once were held a prisoner
  In a castle grim and grey—
A "chrysalis" folk called it—
  But you escaped away.

And now you flutter 'mong the flowers,
  A restless roving elf,
Or fold your wings and lie so still—
  A very flower yourself.

Or hoisting high two gauzy sails,
  You softly float away,
Just like a tiny fairy barque
  Bound for a fairy bay.

The bees must work, the birds must sing,
  The flowers yield perfumes rare;
But you were born a trifler,
  Frail thing of light and air!

WHEN AND WHERE

I WONDER "when" and I wonder "where"
   The Angel of Death will come,
And, laying a finger on lids and lips,
   Will strike me blind and dumb.

I wonder "when" and I wonder "where"!
   Like the skeleton at the feast,
'Mid laughter and mirth this thought finds birth
   Where it is welcome least.

I wonder "when" and I wonder "where"—
   In my prime or old age hoar,
At home, with my loved ones round my bed,
   Or alone on an alien shore.

When and Where

I wonder "when" and I wonder "where!"
   Is God not over all?
He knows the time and He knows the place
   Who marks a sparrow's fall.

WHEN LOVE IS YOUNG

The red and russet of Autumn die,
In the lap of winter their ashes lie,
And the earth is wan and grey the sky.

But the noon of a wondrous joy is mine,
And my pulses thrill with the glowing wine
That flows from the grape of Love's deathless vine.

What care have I that the brown stems bear
Nor leaf nor bloom, and the mad winds tear
The last poor tatters the forests wear?

Is not the heart in mine own glad breast
A garden of roses, a haven of rest,
A bird that has builded a warm love-nest?

A CHARACTER SKETCH

WOMANLY-SWEET in all her ways,
Slow to condemn, and swift to praise;
Ready to help in hour of need,
Generous in thought as well as deed.

Pitiful, tender, yet firm and strong
To uphold the right and put down wrong;
Never a thought of self or gain,
Proud of her God-given gifts—not vain.

Laughter-loving, and fond of fun,
When the "daily round" and task are done;
Modest and maidenly, yet no prude;
Perfect enough, but not "too good."

Half an angel, yet wholly human;
No ideal—a living woman.

FRIENDS

WE are such friends, my little girl and I,
   That, though her summers number scarcely nine
I need none other, as I go my ways
   With her small fingers closely clasping mine.

A little world we two make of our own,
   And people it with all things fair and sweet;
The stars that twinkle overhead at night
   Drop down at dawn in daisies at our feet.

My smiles are hers;—my tears are all my own,
   I keep my sighs and give her all my song,
Because she is so trusting and so weak
   I feel that I can suffer and be strong.

The while I try to keep the narrow way,
   'Tis wide enough for both. And my white dove,
With untried wings, knows little love but this,
   That "Mother" is another name for "Love."

BED-TIME

THE sleepy daisies have said " Good night,"
And tied up their wee frilled nightcaps tight.
The summer day's been hot and long
And daisies, although they are so strong,
Are always tired and ready for bed
Ere the stars, heaven's daisies, awake o'erhead.

The roses have rocked themselves to sleep.
Awake they could no longer keep—
They've been astir since the dawn of day,
Sighing their sweet perfume away,
And feeding the hungry beggar bees
That never say "thanks" nor "if you please!"

And, baby darling, 'tis time that you
Had shut your drowsy eyes of blue—
Wee busy hands, wee busy feet
Must rest sometime, you know, my sweet—
The flower-bells *all* have chimed "Good night."
They'll ring to wake you with the light.

www.ingramcontent.com/pod-product-compliance
Lightning Source LLC
Chambersburg PA
CBHW020143170426
43199CB00010B/868